City Shapes

Ovals

By Jennifer S. Burke

Welcome Books

Children's Press
A Division of Grolier Publishing
New York / London / Hong Kong / Sydney
Danbury, Connecticut

Photo Credits: Cover, p. 5, 11, 19, 21 by Angela Booth; p. 7 © Imagebank; p. 9, 13 © Corbis; p. 15, 17, 21 © Indexstock
Contributing Editor: Mark Beyer
Book Design: Michael DeLisio

Visit Children's Press on the Internet at:
http://publishing.grolier.com

Cataloging-in-Publication Data

Burke, Jennifer S.
    Ovals / by Jennifer S. Burke.
     p. cm. — (City shapes)
    Includes bibliographical references and index.
    Summary: Simple text and pictures of everyday objects introduce oval shapes.
    ISBN 0-516-23076-X (lib. bdg.) — ISBN 0-516-23001-8 (pbk.)
    1. Ovals—Juvenile literature [1. Ovals]
    I. Title. II. Series.
     2000   00-031747
    516'.15—dc21

Contents

1 An Oval Number 4

2 Ovals in a Window 10

3 A Big Oval 12

4 New Words 22

5 To Find Out More 23

6 Index 24

7 About the Author 24

Oval shapes sometimes help to make numbers.

What number does this oval shape help to make?

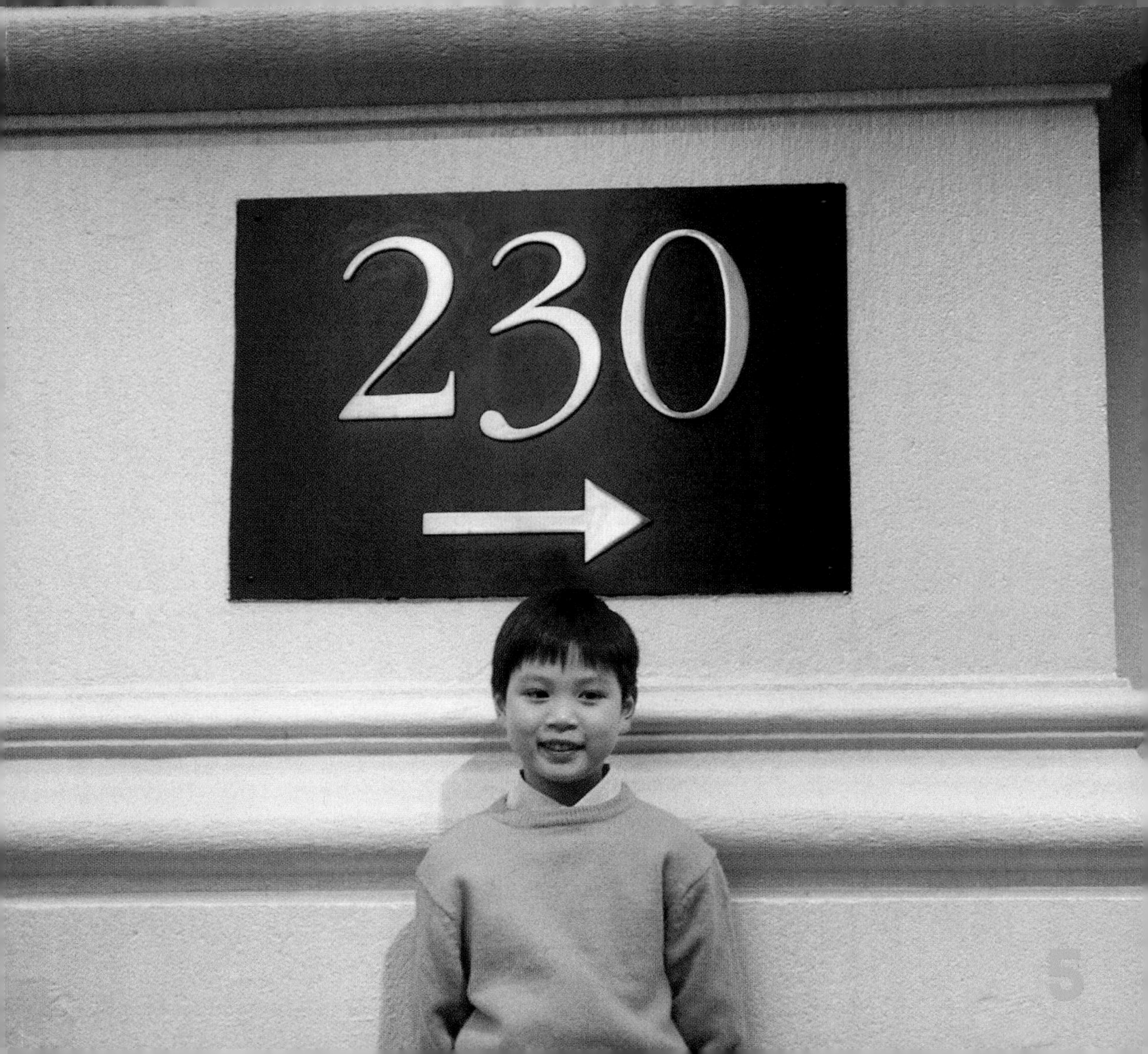
230

Look down at the city!

It is night.

Do you see the **bright** oval?

7.

Some ovals can be **mirrors**.

You can see a **scene** in a mirror.

What do you see in this oval mirror?

9

There are many shapes in this window.

You can see squares and rectangles.

Where are the ovals?

OPTOMETRISTS
ENTRANCE ➡

TLC THE LASER CENTER INC
AFFILIATE
TLC
SEE SEIKO

11

Some ovals are very big.

Pillars hold up this big oval.

13

Some ovals light up at night.

This oval is a **Ferris wheel**.

The Ferris wheel goes around and around.

15

You can find ovals in a playground.

Can you find the ovals behind me?

17

These oval shapes are used to open the doors.

Can you draw the oval shapes using your finger?

Ovals can be big and bright.

Ovals can be small, too.

Ovals in the city are everywhere.

New Words

bright (**bryt**) giving off a lot of light

Ferris wheel (**Fer**-is **weel**) a big wheel that holds people and spins around

mirrors (**mir**-erz) pieces of glass that you can see something in

pillars (**pil**-erz) poles that stand up in the ground to hold things high

scene (**seen**) a place you see where something happens

To Find Out More

Books
Colors and Shapes
by David A. Carter
Simon & Schuster Children's

Colors, Shapes, and Sizes
by Beth A. Wise
McClanahan Book Company

Ovals
by Mary Elizabeth Salzmann
ABDO Publishing Company

Index

bright, 6, 20

Ferris wheel, 14

mirrors, 8

number, 4

pillars, 12
playground, 16

rectangles, 10

scene, 8
squares, 10

About the Author

Jennifer S. Burke is a teacher and a writer living in New York City. She holds a master's degree in reading education from Queens College, New York.

Reading Consultants

Kris Flynn, Coordinator, Small School District Literacy, The San Diego County Office of Education

Shelly Forys, Certified Reading Recovery Specialist, W.J. Zahnow Elementary School, Waterloo, IL

Peggy McNamara, Professor, Bank Street College of Education, Reading and Literacy Program

DATE DUE